OVER IT,

DEVOTIONAL FOR TEEN GIRLS
TRADING COMPARISON FOR THE TRUE ME

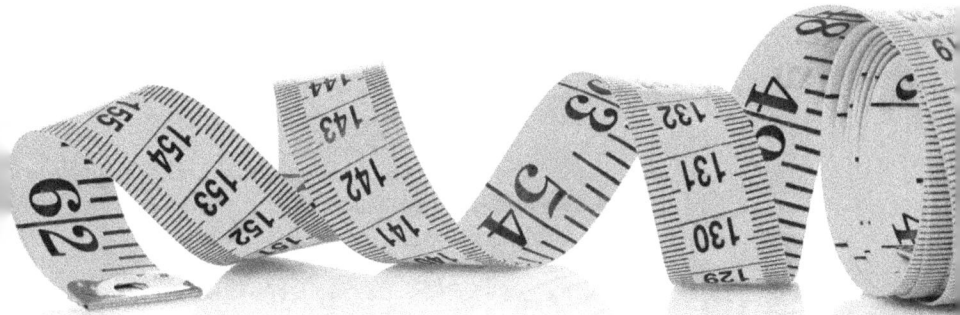

KRISTINE BROWN

To every girl who walked through the door of my classroom, for letting me be part of your story. Though you're older now, you'll always be my girls. *Thank you.*

What's Inside

WEEK
ONE

Day 1
A LOOK IN THE VANITY MIRROR

But if you're content to be simply yourself,
you will become more than yourself.

— LUKE 14:11 MSG

I'D BEEN WAITING FOR THIS DAY FOR MONTHS, AND IT FINALLY CAME!
A week away from home, learning all about fashion, makeup application, and even how to walk down a runway. (If I should ever need that information. You never know, right?) The feelings of anticipation built up inside me like a helium-filled balloon. Little did I know that balloon was about to burst with one final breath.

"What do you like *least* about yourself?" the instructor asked.

The unexpected question hung in the air for what seemed like hours. In reality, it took me only a few seconds to stare myself down in the lighted vanity mirror and begin picking out my flaws.

You see, I wasn't alone sitting in front of that mirror. A vanity mirror is long, usually spanning the whole length of the wall. Ten other girls sat with me, examining their own features. I glanced to the right, then to the left. Striking features stood out—curly blonde hair, dark olive skin, long eyelashes. Without warning, everything my eyes absorbed fused into one condemning thought.

"I don't like my nose," I whispered in response, hoping the other girls in the class didn't hear me.

And with those few words, the voice of comparison settled into my heart.

It's tough to look at ourselves without noticing everything we think is wrong. What's even harder is realizing that when God looks at us, He sees everything *right*. But it's the truth—He does. And when we seal that truth in our hearts, we take away comparison's power.

> *"But if you're content to be simply yourself, you will become more than yourself."*
>
> — LUKE 14:11 MSG

In the fourteenth chapter of Luke, Jesus visited the house of a very important person. As the guests sat down to dinner, Jesus noticed something. Everyone was trying to get a seat near the front. Jesus loved telling stories to teach a lesson, and this day was no different. Jesus gave this advice:

"When you are invited to a wedding feast, don't sit in the seat of honor. What if someone who is more distinguished than you has also been invited? The host will come and say, 'Give this person your seat.' Then you will be embarrassed, and you will have to take whatever seat is left at the foot of the table! Instead, take the lowest place at the foot of the table. Then when your host sees you, he will come and say, 'Friend, we have a better place for you!' Then you will be honored in front of all the other guests" (Luke 14:8-10).

In those days, people with a higher position in society were given a seat closer to the host, a place of honor. Can you imagine walking in a room and trying to figure out where you belong? You feel all eyes fix on you as your face begins to burn. You wonder if they're whispering about you—or maybe even thinking you shouldn't be there at all—when just before you run for the door, the host walks in.

He has a special place prepared for you, right next to him.

You see, God doesn't care about all that high-society stuff, so we don't need to compare ourselves. How God sees us determines our identity. Today, let's erase comparison from our minds and memorize this faith statement.

WHEN WE LOOK AT OURSELVES AND SEE MEDIOCRE, GOD LOOKS AT US AND SEES MAGNIFICENT.

Have you ever looked at another girl and felt *less than* her— less pretty, less talented, less important? You're not alone. The voice of comparison loves to visit God's precious daughters and try to convince us to dislike who we are.

I should know because I battled that voice for years. That's why the conversation with the cosmetics instructor that day marked a huge turning point in my life. After my embarrassing confession, she suggested I get my nose fixed surgically –and for a moment, I considered it. Then God reminded me of today's faith statement in a powerful way (but that's a story for another day).

Beautiful girl, remember this—not only when you glance in the mirror, but every single moment. When you look at yourself and see mediocre, God looks at you and sees magnificent.

Day 2
STEPPING OUT OF HER SHADOW

Your eyes saw my substance, being yet unformed...
— PSALM 139:16 NKJV

THE PRETTIEST GIRL IN 8TH GRADE STOOD NEAR THE CONCESSION
stand, surrounded by a huge group of friends. Boys swarmed
around her like bees to the first flower of springtime. This was a
common gathering place at the Friday night high school football game—just behind the bleachers next to the big, concrete
wall.

Tonight, the boys worked harder than usual to get her attention. Each one took a turn attempting to climb that wall. No
doubt she would be impressed by any guy standing at the top
like king of the mountain. I couldn't help but wonder, "Why
did she get all the attention? What was so special about her?" I
didn't have the answers, but I wanted some of that attention. I
was only a 7th grader. To shift the focus off her and onto me, I
knew what I had to do.

I decided to scale that wall myself.

I had to prove I could climb as good as any boy—even *better*. I pushed past the crowd, and with shoulders back and chin high, I scaled that wall.

But I would soon learn a painful lesson about drawing attention to myself.

> *"Your eyes saw my substance, being yet unformed…"*
> — PSALM 139:16 NKJV

God created each of us for a special purpose, but it's difficult to discover that purpose when our focus is on someone else. A young girl named Hagar knew exactly how that felt. (Her story can be found in Genesis chapters 16 and 21.) Hagar became handmaid to a beautiful lady named Sarai. In those days, if a woman could not become pregnant, the handmaid would be given to the husband to bear children. Although God had promised Sarai that she would have a child, Sarai gave Hagar to her husband Abraham, and Hagar soon became pregnant with a son.

Day after day, Hagar lived the simple life of a servant while Sarai shined as Abraham's wife. Why did Sarai deserve all the attention while Hagar faded into the shadows, completely unnoticed? Those thoughts turned Hagar's heart bitter.

> *"When she knew she was pregnant, she (Hagar) began to despise her mistress."*
>
> — GENESIS 16:4 NIV

Hagar had enough; she was over it. Frustrated and confused, she ran away. It was in that moment when God became *El Roi* to Hagar, "the God who sees me."

> *"The angel of the Lord found Hagar beside a spring of water in the wilderness, along the road to Shur. The angel said to her, 'Hagar, Sarai's servant, where have you come from, and where are you going?' 'I'm running away from my mistress, Sarai,' she replied. The angel of the Lord said to her, 'Return to your mistress, and submit to her authority'."*
>
> — GENESIS 16:7-9

God had a plan, but Hagar needed to trust. She needed to quit focusing on Sarai and look to God instead. The lesson she learned that day is one we need to grasp too. It can be summed up in this faith statement.

WHEN I FOCUS MY GAZE ON GOD, I WILL FIND MY TRUE WORTH.

Do you sometimes catch yourself doubting your own abilities? Have you ever wondered why another girl seems to have the spotlight while you stand unnoticed in the shadows? If you have any doubts about your worth, God answers that doubt in today's verse from Psalm 139:16. We have *substance*. We are *noticed*. We are *seen*.

If I had paused to consider my Creator that fateful night at the football game, I may have saved myself the embarrassment that followed my stunt. My foot slipped, and down I slid. Big-time fail! Thankfully I only skinned my leg; things could've been much worse.

Beautiful girl, there's no need to shine a spotlight on yourself. (And I don't recommend climbing dangerous walls, either!) When you focus your gaze on God, you will find your true worth.

Idea! Use the journaling space on pg. 37 to write your thoughts about today's verse.

Day 3
DISCOVERING GOD'S PROMISES FOR YOU

Now you are no longer a slave but God's own child.
And since you are His child. God has made you His heir.

— GALATIANS 4:7

YOUNG, PREGNANT, WORKING A JOB THAT WASN'T HER CHOICE FOR A woman who treated her poorly—Hagar's situation went beyond difficult to downright awful. What did she do to deserve such treatment?

In yesterday's devotion, we left off when an angel of the Lord visited Hagar in her most desperate moment. God made Himself known to Hagar for the first time, but that wasn't the end of Hagar's story. She needed help, but she had no one. Just when things looked the darkest for Hagar, God made her a profound promise.

"The angel of the Lord said to her, 'Return to your mistress, and submit to her authority.' Then he added, 'I will give you more descendants than you can count.'"

GENESIS 16:9-10

God had something special planned for Hagar, but she needed to keep her heart tuned in to Him in order to hear His promise. Hagar and Sarai were both guilty of mistreating each other. In fact, their constant conflict with each other caused big problems. That happens to us sometimes too. We stare at our problems instead of setting our eyes on the God who promises to take care of us.

"Now you are no longer a slave but God's own child. And since you are His child. God has made you His heir."

— GALATIANS 4:7

Right now, you might be asking yourself, "So how do I recognize God's promise for me? Will I hear His voice speaking to me?" An angel visited Hagar to deliver God's message, but that may not be the case for us. Thankfully, we have a book full of God's promises that we can turn to every day—our Bible. Reading Scripture is the same as hearing God speak to us because God and His Word are one and the same. (See John 1:1).

We are God's children. That will never change as long as we believe in Jesus and keep Him close. Isn't that awesome? As we continue learning God's promises for us, we won't need to compare ourselves anymore. This leads us to our faith statement for today.

HOLDING ONTO GOD'S PROMISES HELPS US LET GO OF COMPARISON.

Things didn't turn around right away for Hagar. Remember, she still had to go back to Sarai. It would be many years before she saw her promise fulfilled, but she learned a valuable lesson that we should learn too. When we live according to the truth above, we won't worry about measuring up to someone else. We can start living our best life knowing God has something special for us, even if our current circumstances look rough.

Beautiful girl, you are God's child. Holding onto that promise* will help you let go of comparison.

---

* For printable lists of God's promises, visit ***kristinebrown.net.***

Day 4
SCROLLING, STREAMING, AND STORIES

I will never leave you nor forsake you.

— HEBREWS 13:5 ESV

HAS SOMEONE EVER SPREAD AN UGLY RUMOR ABOUT YOU? OR HAS someone blasted a hurtful comment toward you on social media? Then you will relate to what happened next in Hagar's journey, after she returned to her job serving Sarai. They didn't have smartphones back then, but women in the Bible had to deal with mean girls in their day too.

Several years had passed since Hagar gave birth to her baby, Ishmael, and all that time, Hagar dealt with Sarai's jealousy. But Hagar knew she was where God told her to be, so she stayed. Then just as God promised, Sarai also gave birth to a baby boy.

"And Sarah declared, 'God has brought me laughter. All who hear about this will laugh with me. Who would have said to Abraham that Sarah would nurse a baby? Yet I have given Abraham a son in his old age!'"

— GENESIS 21:6-7

With the entrance of baby Isaac into the world came even more tension between Sarah and Hagar. Ishmael was the oldest son, and Sarah didn't like that one bit. One day, in a fit of meanness, Sarah told Abraham to send Hagar and Ishmael away for good. They didn't have social media in those days, but just think what kind of posts would have resulted from all that bitterness.

"So she turned to Abraham and demanded, 'Get rid of that slave woman and her son. He is not going to share the inheritance with my son, Isaac. I won't have it!'"

— GENESIS 21:10

So Abraham obeyed, leaving Hagar and Ishmael to wander alone in the wilderness. Hopelessness took over as Hagar watched her son nearing death. She laid him down and walked away. She let her loneliness draw her deeper into despair instead of drawing her closer to God. That happens to us sometimes too.

Hate, put-downs, and rumors can make us feel alone, like we don't have any friends—especially when they appear on our phone screens for all to see. Then everyone else gets to add their own comments to the conversation, making matters much worse. When loneliness happens, we try to fill time with distractions. Binge-watching a new series, scrolling on our phones, and watching other people's 'stories' all seem to provide temporary relief. But even though screen time can be fun, these distractions can actually take us *deeper* into that loneliness we're trying to avoid. The truth is that the more time we spend on social media, the more alone we feel. And that's not what God wants for us.

Alone time can be a blessing when we use that time to talk to God. His presence provides comfort unlike anything we can find elsewhere. When we put down our phones and let ourselves be still with Him, our mood will change in a miraculous way. Our faith statement for today is this.

THINGS LOOK BRIGHTER WHEN WE TURN OUR ALONE TIME INTO A CONVERSATION WITH GOD.

In Hagar's sadness, had she forgotten God's powerful promise? Had she let all the mistreatment cause her to give up? Maybe time alone was just what Hagar needed to hear God's beautiful voice once again. His Word says, "I will never leave you nor forsake you" (Hebrews 13:5 ESV). He hadn't abandoned her, and He will never abandon you and me.

God made a promise to Hagar, and in the middle of her struggle, He worked a miracle to show her how special she was to Him.

"But God heard the boy crying, and the angel of God called to Hagar from heaven, "Hagar, what's wrong? Do not be afraid! God has heard the boy crying as he lies there. Go to him and comfort him, for I will make a great nation from his descendants."

— GENESIS 21:17-18

Let's take our lesson from Hagar today. When we feel forsaken, let's remember God's promise that He will always be with us.

Beautiful girl, when scrolling, streaming, and stories leave you feeling lonely, try putting distractions down and talking to God instead. Because things do look brighter when we turn alone time into a conversation with God.

Idea! As you talk to God this week, turn to pgs. 35-39 & spend some time being creative with God's truth. Color the quote, write a prayer, or doodle from your heart.

Day 5
ANOTHER GLANCE IN THE VANITY MIRROR

And since we are his children, we are his heirs...

— ROMANS 8:17

I'D LIKE TO VENTURE BACK TO DAY ONE WHERE I LEFT US SITTING IN front of the vanity mirror. There's more to that story, and it's finally time for me to tell you what happened next.

God had something special in mind for me. He always does. And in true God-fashion, He revealed His message in an extraordinary way. Remember the instructor's question during my week at modeling and fashion school?

"Why don't you just get a nose job?"

I didn't have to think about it for long. I blurted out my response: "Because my mom wouldn't allow it!"

I knew my mother would never approve. I was only a teen after all. I also knew I should've been proud of my nose; it's a family trait. My mother, grandfather, and most likely generations before him all had the same nose shape. Honestly, I felt too embarrassed to tell my mom about the conversation. I didn't want to hurt her feelings. Plus, my nose never bothered me before. At least, I *thought* it hadn't.

Arriving home at the end of a long week, I decided to confess what happened to my mom and her best friend. Coincidentally, Mom's friend has a similar nose, so much so that they're often mistaken for sisters when they're together. I spilled it all. Every painful detail— from how pretty all the girls were to the instructor's question about my flaws. Then mom's friend said something I'll never forget:

"Why would you ever consider changing your nose?" Mom's friend asked. "It's a sign of royalty."

Royalty.

She explained that in early Victorian England, men and women with a bump on the bridge of the nose were instantly recognized. The Aquiline nose, as it was called, was the most highly regarded of all nose types! Back then, when you saw someone with the distinguishable bump, you knew she was from noble birth.

Here's our final faith statement of the week.

IN THE MIDDLE OF MY DOUBT, GOD REMINDS ME OF MY ROYAL POSITION AS HIS CHILD.

Now isn't that just like our loving God? Through the hurt of our insecurity, He reveals our worth. Still doubting how the God of all creation could accept you into His royal lineage? You don't have to take my word for it. Instead, allow me to point you to the unquestionable truth...

"And since we are his children, we are his heirs..."
— ROMANS 8:17

From that day forward, I began learning to embrace my imperfections. To see myself the way God designed me and think of myself according to His words instead of my own. Learning to see ourselves the way God sees us is a habit. We need to practice it, whatever age we are. The more we think about the amazing things He says about us, the more we will *believe it.* God started changing my heart—and trust me, He can change yours, too.

Beautiful girl, in the midst of all that doubt, let God remind you of your royal position. You are His child. Nothing can change who you are.

WHEN we look at
OURSELVES
and see
MEDIOCRE
GOD
looks at US
and sees
MAGNIFICENT

Journal

Doodle

WEEK
TWO

Day 6
WHO DO I SEE LOOKING BACK AT ME?

So since we find ourselves fashioned into all these excellently formed and marvelously functioning parts in Christ's body, let's just go ahead and be what we were made to be, without enviously or pridefully comparing ourselves with each other, or trying to be something we aren't.

— ROMANS 12:5-6 MSG

HAVE YOU NOTICED HOW MANY MIRRORS YOU SEE EVERY DAY? SOME of us even carry one around in our back pocket. Checking our hair or outfit is as easy as pulling out a phone. Girls today have more opportunities to catch their reflection than generations before us. But when we catch our reflection, we may also catch ourselves *reflecting* too much on what we see.

One of my all-time favorite book and movie characters had a life-changing encounter with a mirror, just like I did. Her name is Lucy.

In the movie *Voyage of the Dawn Treader*, based on the book from the *Chronicles of Narnia* series by C.S. Lewis, Lucy Pevensie and her siblings go on a quest to save Narnia, their former home. In this tale, Lucy—along with her brother Edmund and cousin Eustace—set sail on a majestic ship for the voyage of a lifetime. Along the way, shadows of doubt try to cast defeat into the young warriors' hearts.

In one scene, Lucy expresses her inner desire to be like her beautiful older sister, Susan. Lucy rises from her bed in the middle of the night to look into a magical mirror, hoping her wish will come true. As she gazes at herself, a transformation takes place. She sees Susan instead of her own reflection!

Lucy is drawn into an imaginary scene where only her sister and brothers exist—a world where she *is* her sister.

Lucy wished herself away, without even knowing it.

She is then whisked back to her room, but this time Aslan, the wise lion, stands by her side.

Lucy: "I just wanted to be beautiful like Susan. That's all."

Aslan: "You wished yourself away, and with it much more. Your brothers and sister wouldn't know Narnia without you, Lucy. You discovered it first, remember?"

Lucy: "I'm so sorry."

Aslan: "You doubt your value. Don't run from who you are."

Aslan represents the voice of truth in Lucy's life. And just like Lucy, we too have a Voice of Truth when we question our worth.

DAY 6: WHO DO I SEE LOOKING BACK AT ME? ■ 45

"So since we find ourselves fashioned into all these excellently formed and marvelously functioning parts in Christ's body, let's just go ahead and be what we were made to be, without enviously or pridefully comparing ourselves with each other, or trying to be something we aren't."

— Romans 12:5-6 MSG

In her longing to be like Susan, Lucy failed to see the beauty within herself. She didn't realize the unique contribution she made to her friends, family, and world. This brings us to our faith statement for today.

THE WORLD IS A BETTER PLACE WHEN WE EMBRACE WHO GOD CREATED US TO BE.

When you look at your reflection, who is looking back? Do you sometimes catch yourself reflecting on someone you'd rather be?

Just for fun, let's try something. The next time we catch ourselves searching for a mirror, let's stop. Instead, let's spend that time reflecting on our Creator. We will be amazed at how awesome it feels to think about ourselves through the eyes of God

Beautiful girl, the world would be an empty place without your unique reflection in it.

Day 7
GOD CREATED YOUR SPARKLE

For you created my inmost being;
you knit me together in my mother's womb.

— PSALM 139:13 NIV

I HAVE THIS FRIEND. HER NAME IS STANDARD, AND I'VE KNOWN HER for most of my life.

In high school, Standard didn't just *sit* at the cool table, she *was* the cool table. In my opinion, she had it all. I tried my best to copy her every move. When she sported her new summer tan, so did I. I dyed my hair to match her golden locks. Whatever trend she set, I followed.

Standard isn't an actual person—not in the physical sense anyway. She's a character we create in our minds—a perfect mixture of every pin, post, and picture we see. They all blend together into this image to measure ourselves against. And when we compare ourselves to something so unreal, we end up focusing on our flaws. But that's not what God wants for us.

If Standard sounds familiar, you're not alone. Girls throughout history have felt like they didn't measure up A woman in Scripture named Leah knew exactly how that felt. She lived her life feeling outshined by her sister Rachel.

"There was no sparkle in Leah's eyes, but Rachel had a beautiful figure and a lovely face."

— GENESIS 29:17

Remember Abraham and Sarah from Hagar's story? Their son Isaac lived to be an old man and have two sons, Esau and Jacob. Isaac sent Jacob on a journey to find a wife from the tribe of his Uncle Laban. When Jacob got there, he saw the beautiful Rachel and instantly fell in love. After seven years, Laban agreed to let the two lovebirds marry.

But Laban had an older daughter named Leah, and in the verse above, we discover an important detail about her.

She hid her sparkle.

I can totally relate. Can you? Day after day watching all eyes turn toward your sister or friend when she walks into a room. Resolving to be 'plain-old-Leah' forever because—why try? Thankfully, God didn't see her as 'plain-old-Leah'. And He doesn't see us that way either.

"For you created my inmost being; you knit me together in my mother's womb."

— PSALM 139:13 NIV

God not only designed our physical features—everything from the shape of our nose to the color of our skin. He crafted the deepest parts of us, who we are on the inside. That's where our sparkle begins. If we spend too much time hanging out with Standard, we keep our sparkle hidden away. We tuck the best of ourselves deep inside and show the world something phony instead.

Today's verse tells us a valuable truth. God "created our *inmost* being." The part hidden away. The best part of us. Our faith statement for today is this.

GOD CREATED YOUR SPARKLE. IT'S THE BEST PART OF WHO YOU ARE.

In an interesting turn of events, Jacob ended up with both Rachel and Leah as wives after a 14-year stay working for his uncle. We will get to that story another day, but for now, let's smile at the thought of God giving us each a unique sparkle as the essence of our true selves. I feel a little brighter already!

Beautiful girl, you are not outshined by anyone else. Let that sparkle show.

Day 8

#FEELINGUNLOVED

We know how much God loves us, and we have put our trust in his love. God is love, and all who live in love live in God, and God lives in them.

— 1 JOHN 4:16

HAVE YOU EVER BEEN SITTING IN CLASS WHEN YOUR TEACHER AN-nounces you'll be working with a partner that day? She scans the room looking for her first set of victims. Everyone scoots down in their seats, hoping to turn invisible as she assigns one set of part-ners, then the next, then the next.

She calls your name and pairs you with the cutest boy in class! But then you notice a strange look on his face and wonder if he'd rather work with someone else. Comparison shows up un-invited once again.

This may be how Leah felt when Jacob planned to marry Ra-chel first but ended up with Leah as his wife instead. Laban agreed to let Jacob marry Rachel after working for his uncle seven years. But on the wedding night, Laban secretly sent Leah with her face covered so Jacob couldn't see who it was. Imagine the look on Jacob's face when he discovered Leah under that bridal veil instead of his beautiful fiancé Rachel!

Then imagine how that must've made Leah feel. Completely unloved.

> *"We know how much God loves us, and we have put our trust in his love. God is love, and all who live in love live in God, and God lives in them."*
>
> — I JOHN 4:16

God designed us for love, but He also wants us to come to *Him* to fill that desire. If we expect others to meet that need in our lives, we will never be satisfied. Unlike the temporary dose of love people have to offer, God's love will fill our heart until it overflows, spilling His love onto everyone around us.

God saw how unloved Leah felt, so He did something about it. He gave her a special gift.

> *"When the Lord saw that Leah was unloved, he enabled her to have children, but Rachel could not conceive."*
>
> — GENESIS 29:31

Even when we don't see anything special within ourselves, God works miracles to show us how special we are to Him. This blessing showed Leah an important truth about God's love.

WE NEVER HAVE TO FEEL UNLOVED, BECAUSE GOD WILL ALWAYS LOVE US—NO MATTER WHAT.

Maybe you can relate to Leah's feelings of rejection. Maybe a boy hurt you, or maybe the people who were supposed to love and take care of you let you down. Wherever these unloved feelings started, they can end today with a newfound love—*a better one.*

If you're feeling unloved today, know this. There is nothing stronger, nothing greater, nothing more powerful than the love of God. I wish I could jump right through the page and give you a great big hug and share that love with you. But the good news is you don't need me in order to experience it. He is right there with you at this very moment, wrapping you in a hug more comforting than anything you've ever felt. Take a minute to sense His comforting presence.

Beautiful girl, anytime you feel unloved, turn your eyes toward God. He will always, always love you. No matter what.

Day 9
MAY I HAVE YOUR ATTENTION, PLEASE?

We know, dear brothers and sisters, that God loves you and has chosen you to be his own people.

— 1 Thessalonians 1:4

JACOB MAY NOT HAVE LOVED HER BEFORE, BUT LEAH FELT CERTAIN HE would love her *now.*

"So Leah became pregnant and gave birth to a son. She named him Reuben, for she said, 'The Lord has noticed my misery, and now my husband will love me."

— Genesis 29:32

God responded to Leah's discouragement with the unmatched blessing of having children, but it wasn't enough. Leah still longed for her husband's attention. And this need grew with each new baby. After Reuben came Simeon, then her third son, Levi. Notice how Leah's appetite for affection from Jacob grew more urgent.

"Then she became pregnant a third time and gave birth to another son. He was named Levi, for she said, 'Surely this time my husband will feel affection for me, since I have given him three sons!'"

— GENESIS 29:34

Leah let her worth be determined by someone else other than God. She thought her only hope for winning Jacob's love would be to give him something he didn't have—children. But God had a greater purpose in giving Leah children. She just needed to see Him as the source of her worth, instead of someone else.

"We know, dear brothers and sisters, that God loves you and has chosen you to be his own people."

— 1 THESSALONIANS 1:4

Chosen *you.*

We all know what it's like to want someone's attention. Whether it's attention from our parents, the coach of our team, or a boy we like, relying on another person to give us what we seek will only leave us feeling emptier than ever. Turning our attention to God instead of striving to please others shows God our willingness to seek His will. That brings us to today's faith statement.

WE FIND OUR WORTH IN GOD'S WORDS, NOT ATTENTION FROM OTHERS.

Leah finally realized God had a greater plan for her. It took time, but her perspective changed with the birth of her fourth son, Judah.

"Once again Leah became pregnant and gave birth to another son. She named him Judah, for she said, 'Now I will praise the Lord!'"

— GENESIS 29:35

What did Leah do differently after Judah was born?

That's right. She didn't turn to her husband to see if he was paying attention. She decided to praise the Lord. Leah didn't even know that one day Judah and his brothers would grow up to become the foundation of the twelve tribes of Israel. Amazing! Leah wanted these babies to draw her husband's love toward her, but God's love would one day fulfill a great plan for all people, including you and me.

When we're tempted to seek attention from others, let's remember that God is attentive to our every need. It doesn't matter what anyone else thinks. God's opinion of us is the only one that counts, and that's enough.

Beautiful girl, God has chosen you. Take a deep breath and relax, knowing your worth is not found in what others see in you, but what God sees.

Idea! Use the journaling space on pg. 65 to make a list of your unique qualities: strengths, talents, & personality traits. Think about how God created you for a special purpose.

Day 10
SISTERS DIVIDED

Since God chose you to be the holy people he loves, you must clothe yourselves with tenderhearted mercy, kindness, humility, gentleness, and patience.

— COLOSSIANS 3:12

GROWING UP, MY SISTER AND I HAD OUR OWN ROOMS. THAT MEANT I had a space all to myself! You'd think we would've been thankful to have a quiet place to retreat to whenever we wanted. But sometimes we took things for granted.

One day we got super bored and decided sharing a room would be a great idea. My mom tried to talk us out of it, but she finally conceded. I think she knew what would happen. Sometimes I just didn't listen! Once we moved our things in together and arranged it all just right, my mom wasn't surprised at all by what we did next.

We stretched a piece of masking tape right down the middle. Our new togetherness became divided.

"Since God chose you to be the holy people he loves, you must

clothe yourselves with tenderhearted mercy, kindness, humility, gentleness, and patience."

— COLOSSIANS 3:12

Jesus showed us by example how to treat others. He was a friend to everyone when He walked on this earth, and He's still our best friend today. After Jesus went to heaven to be with God, Paul taught Jesus' followers how to live, like in the above verse. Mercy, kindness, humility, gentleness, and patience. I guess you'd call Jesus the trendsetter when it came to treating others well.

Sharing space is tough, and I'm not just talking about 'room' space. Friendship, time, and life in general all count as *space* too. Have you ever thought about who you share your space with? Who do you treat as a friend, spend time with, or do life with? Of course, it's important to use wisdom with our space. Not everyone needs to be a friend (especially where social media is concerned). But sometimes with other girls our age, we create dividing lines without even knowing it.

The new girl at school who sits by herself in the cafeteria at lunch. Your younger sibling who just wants to hang out with you. The kid in the youth group at church who never gets invited. All these examples show opportunity for us to display the character Paul describes in today's verse. Remember this faith statement.

SINCE WE ARE GOD'S GIRLS, LET'S BE SISTERS UNITED INSTEAD OF SISTERS DIVIDED.

What I wouldn't give to have those days back sharing a room with my sister! I would handle things a lot differently, that's for sure.

In what ways can you show these character traits to other girls around you? As you pray, who comes to mind? Wherever you are today, God will give you a chance to form a friendship with a sister in Christ.

Beautiful girl, God is calling you to be a sister united.

GOD

CREATED

your

Sparkle

JOURNAL

Doodle

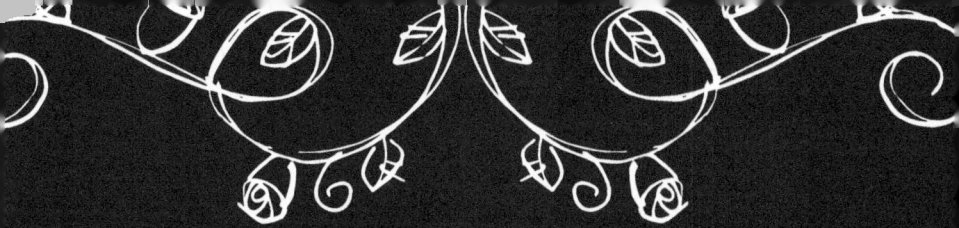

WEEK
THREE

Day 11
GOING THROUGH HARD THINGS

I have told you these things, so that in me you may have peace.
In this world you will have trouble. But take heart!
I have overcome the world.

—JOHN 16:33 NIV

WITHOUT WARNING, MY BEST FRIEND BECAME VERY SICK. BY THE
time the doctors figured out what was wrong, they estimated she
had only a few months to live.

That next Sunday at church, we sat beside each other as we always did. I'm glad we had a few moments together. I knew it was a
special gift for two special friends. We shared our feelings about our
years of friendship, holding nothing back. I'll never forget that day.
Because even though we both thought we had months or even weeks
left to prepare for her passing, she died the following Sunday.

I've tried to write about what it felt like losing my friend. I
thought if I somehow put it into words, it would help others understand the pain. But the thing is, you most likely already understand
the pain of dealing with hard things. Everyone does. Our struggles

may not look the same, but we all have them. That's one thing people have in common. We all go through hardships in this life.

> *"I have told you these things, so that in me you may have peace. In this world you will have trouble. But take heart! I have overcome the world."*
>
> — JOHN 16:33 NIV

When life throws difficulties at me, my first instinct is to ask God, "Why??"

"Why did this have to happen? Why didn't you stop it? Why do bad things happen to good people?"

If you've asked these questions too, you're not alone. God not only knew what we would go through, He knew we would ask, wonder, and seek answers. Because He loves us more than anything, He sent His son Jesus to share the Truth. Today's verse is Jesus' actual voice speaking to His followers—you and me.

Before we look at it again, will you do something for me? Trust me on this. I want you to close your eyes, and picture yourself sitting across from Jesus. Just the two of you. He's leaning in and looking at you with compassion and understanding. He holds your hand and says these words. (Put your name in the blank.)

"_____, in this world you will have trouble."

Now, think about what that means for you. Did something occur in your life that you didn't understand? Something hard that you struggled with? Are you going through a hardship right now?

Then let's continue our conversation with Jesus.

"_____, in this world you will have trouble. But, *take heart!*" (Emphasis mine.)

Take heart! It's as if Jesus is saying, "Everything will be okay. Be encouraged! Stay close to me!" And as we do that, as we hold His hand to walk through the difficulties of life, He promises to be there every step of the way.

God is with us through hard times—giving us strength even when we don't feel it. We grow stronger and learn to depend on God more during the tough things. That brings us to our faith statement.

HARDSHIP PREPARES MY HEART AND HELPS ME DEPEND ON GOD.

We may still wonder why things happen, but we can know this: without hardships, we wouldn't receive the joy that comes from answered prayers and miracle moments (which are awesome, by the way!).

Beautiful girl, as you go through life's hard things, know deep in your heart that the hardships you experience are helping you grow into a deeper relationship with God.

Day 12
HOW TO DEAL WITH HURTFUL COMMENTS

Once when they had finished eating and drinking in Shiloh,
Hannah stood up.

— 1 SAMUEL 1:9 NIV

A YOUNG WOMAN IN SCRIPTURE KNEW WHAT IT WAS LIKE TO FACE hardship. Her name was Hannah, and we can learn a lot from her story. But before we venture all the way back to around 1000 B.C. to meet her, let's take a quick look at the story I shared with you yesterday—the week after my best friend unexpectedly passed away.

Only two days after her death, someone approached me about a conflict between us. Her words were less than nice. Shocked by the whole conversation, I left feeling worse than I had before. *How could she? Didn't she know what I was going through?* Her comments heaped another load of *bad* onto my already overwhelmed shoulders.

Have you ever been in that situation? When you're going through a tough time and someone says something that just makes it worse? Hannah knew this feeling all too well. She wanted a baby more than anything, but "the Lord had closed her womb." (Remember what we learned yesterday about hardships.) To make matters worse, her husband had another wife named Peninnah. And Peninnah's favorite pastime was throwing hurtful words at Hannah.

> *"But her rival wife taunted her cruelly, rubbing it in and never letting her forget that God had not given her children."*
> — 1 SAMUEL 1:6 MSG

This wasn't just a one-time thing either. The teasing went on for *years*. How horrible that must have been for Hannah! It caused so much pain that she "would be reduced to tears and would not even eat" (1 Samuel 1:7). But Hannah was God's girl. She knew deep down God's words about her were the only ones that mattered. So one day, she decided to do something about it.

> *"Once when they had finished eating and drinking in Shiloh, Hannah stood up."*
> — 1 SAMUEL 1:9 NIV

Another translation says she "got up and went to pray." Surprised? If I were in Hannah's situation, I may have thought up the best insult I could and hurled it right back at Peninnah. Or I might even have gathered a group of friends to treat her badly and make her feel the same hurt she had caused me. But not Hannah.

Her example shows us exactly what to do when dealing with mean comments. That brings us to our faith statement for today.

WHEN SOMEONE THROWS MEAN WORDS AT US, WE CAN STAND UP, WALK AWAY, AND PRAY.

Hannah stood up, walked away from the table, marched right into the temple, and prayed from her deep anguish. Want to know something cool? After that prayer, Peninnah's name isn't mentioned again in Scripture. Her words no longer held power over Hannah. When we're hurting, God is the best place to go. He is always ready to hear our prayers.

Beautiful girl, people can be mean. Remember God's opinion of you is the only one that matters. When hurtful comments happen, stand up, walk away, and pray.

*Sometimes meanness can escalate into a bullying situation. If this happens to you, tell a trusted adult in your life what's going on. (A counselor, coach, teacher, or youth pastor.) Ask for their help. You don't have to face it alone.

Day 13
TRADING DOWNCAST FOR HOPEFUL

Why, my soul, are you downcast? Why so disturbed within me?
Put your hope in God, for I will yet praise him,
my Savior and my God.

— PSALM 43:5 NIV

ONE OF MY ALL-TIME FAVORITE TV CHARACTERS IS A SPUNKY GIRL named Sue. As the middle child of three, Sue struggles to find her place in the world. But that doesn't stop her from trying! In fact, she's best known for her optimistic attitude. It's what gives her character from "The Middle" show such a fun, likeable quality.

Sue tries out for one team or activity after another, facing rejection every time. Anyone else would have a moment of sadness or frustration, maybe even give up. But not Sue. I catch myself laughing along as her family searches for words to encourage her, but somehow, she always finds a way to pick herself back up and discover the sunshine behind the clouds.

"Why, my soul, are you downcast? Why so disturbed within me? Put your hope in God, for I will yet praise him, my Savior and my God."

— PSALM 43:5 NIV

Wouldn't it be wonderful to be a little more like Sue when rejection happens? To be able to find the good when things don't go as planned? Let's revisit Hannah's story where we left off yesterday.

Hannah had just made the decision to stand up, walk away, and pray. As we continue, we find her in the temple praying out of great sadness. Hannah likely had feelings like rejection and hopelessness knocking at the door of her heart. She cried out to God, and even Eli the priest heard her. We don't have to hold back our feelings when calling out to our heavenly Father. Check out a portion of the conversation between Hannah and Eli.

"'...I am very discouraged, and I was pouring out my heart to the Lord. Don't think I am a wicked woman! For I have been praying out of great anguish and sorrow.' 'In that case,' Eli said, 'go in peace! May the God of Israel grant the request you have asked of him.' 'Oh, thank you, sir!' she exclaimed. Then she went back and began to eat again, and she was no longer sad.'"

— 1 SAMUEL 1:15-18

The NIV versions says Hannah's face was "no longer downcast." In an instant, Hannah's attitude changed. Together, let's take a closer look at when and how the shift occurred. Grab a pencil, pen, or highlighter, then read the passage above one more time.

With your pen, draw a heart where you sense a change in Hannah. What was happening at that moment? What caused the drastic turnaround? (Idea: Jot down your thoughts on the journal page.)

Hannah was over being downhearted. From that day forward, Hannah held onto hope. She had to. And she would soon discover that God's promises don't always happen right away. That brings us to today's faith statement.

A HOPEFUL ATTITUDE HELPS US WHEN WE'RE TEMPTED TO STAY IN A PLACE OF SADNESS.

Changing our attitude from downcast to hopeful is hard, but Hannah's story shows the power of a hope-filled life. And as an added bonus, God multiplies that positivity when others see us display hope—just like when I watch Sue's optimism as she reacts to adversity. Our joy is contagious.

Beautiful girl, when you feel left out, rejected, or forgotten, turn to God. He will help you discover the hope in your situation. Shifting from downcast to hopeful will erase the temptation to stay sad.

Day 14
THE POWER OF POSITIVE WORDS

Do not use foul or abusive language. Let everything you say be
good and helpful, so that your words will be an encouragement to those
who hear them.

— EPHESIANS 4:29

CAN I GET PERSONAL ABOUT PENINNAH FOR A MINUTE? I IDENTIFY
with her. Knowing me today, you might not see the resemblance.
But I was a different person back then, before the love of God
changed me from the inside out.

Junior high can be a treacherous time for girls. Each one of
us trying to discover who we are and determine our own identity.
During that time in my life, I decided that putting on a tough ex-
terior would shield me from any potential rejection. So I became a
mean girl, hurting feelings and leaving people out.

I confess that I'm ashamed of that person. But thankfully,
through God's grace, I can let go of shame and know He has for-
given me for the mistakes of my past. Looking back at those choic-
es helps me understand what causes people to say mean things.

Sharing the truth with you and revisiting those old feelings shows me what's beneath that hard outer shell some girls put on.

Peninnah wore a hard shell too. Maybe her hate came from seeing her husband Elkanah serve a double portion of food to Hannah every year. Remember what we learned yesterday? Elkanah loved Hannah more. However, even though we try to understand Peninnah's resentment, we shouldn't make excuses for her behavior. Instead, let's see what God teaches about the power of positive words.

> *"Do not use foul or abusive language. Let everything you say be good and helpful, so that your words will be an encouragement to those who hear them."*
>
> — EPHESIANS 4:29

There are many reasons why a young lady might choose to be mean to other girls, but the root cause is often insecurity that she just doesn't know how to process. When we truly grasp who God says we are, we will have no reason to feel bad about ourselves.

Whether you have been on the giving or receiving side of hurtful words, the best thing to do is ask God for guidance and follow the wisdom He gives.

In 1 Peter 3:9, it says this. "Don't retaliate with insults when people insult you. Instead, pay them back with a blessing. That is what God has called you to do, and He will grant you His blessing." Our faith statement for today is this.

GOD CALLS US TO BE A BLESSING, EVEN WHEN OTHERS INSULT US.

Words have power. They can tear people down, or they can build people up. God teaches us that answering bitter words with more bitterness only makes the problem worse. The voice of comparison gets louder when I put others down, but blessing people with words will drown it out.

Let's take our cue from Hannah today and begin by forgiving the *Peninnahs* in our lives. Then let's commit to saying nice things when someone hurts us with their words. We never know the impact God can make when we obey Him.

Beautiful girl, God has called you to be a blessing today. Don't let insults stop you from encouraging others.

Day 15
I HAVE SOMETHING TO TELL YOU!

Let praise flow from my lips.

— PSALM 119:171

IMAGINE FOR A MOMENT THAT YOU'VE JUST RECEIVED THE BEST NEWS ever. In fact, it's so mind-blowing, you can't even believe it! As you sit stunned, trying to process this fabulous news, what do you want to do first?

While you think about your answer to my question, let's see what happened after Hannah received the good news from Eli that God would answer her prayer. When we paused yesterday, Hannah turned her frown around and traded hopelessness for hope. She began the long journey home from the temple holding on to a big promise from God.

> *"And in due time she gave birth to a son. She named him Samuel, for she said, 'I asked the Lord for him.'"*
>
> — 1 SAMUEL 1:20

Yes! God fulfilled His promise! Hannah knew what she had to do. Her enthusiasm was almost more than she could bear. If she kept quiet much longer, she just might burst. She had to tell Eli the priest about her miracle.

> *"Let praise flow from my lips."*
>
> — PSALM 119:171

Remember the scenario I asked you to imagine a few moments ago? Think about how you respond to good news. Do you scream and shout? Jump up and down? Or like Hannah, do you want to tell a friend, someone who will celebrate with you? Now imagine how it would feel if you couldn't tell that person *for several years.* That's how the story progressed with Hannah and Eli. Years passed before she made her way back to the temple, but the time finally came.

> *"'Sir, do you remember me?' Hannah asked. 'I am the very woman who stood here several years ago praying to the Lord. I asked the Lord to give me this boy, and He has granted my request.'"*
>
> — 1 SAMUEL 1:26-27

During those in-between years, it would've been easy for Hannah to forget all about it and enjoy life with her husband and new son. But she knew something important: that pesky comparison monster would love for us to forget about God's blessings. Thanking Him out loud keeps away things like envy and jealousy.

That brings us to today's faith statement.

WE SILENCE THE VOICE OF COMPARISON BY REMEMBERING GOD'S GOODNESS.

Filling our thoughts with God's goodness doesn't leave room for the voice of comparison, even when others tell us we have every right to complain or feel down. You see, while Hannah praised God that day, she also gave her son over to Eli to be raised at the temple— the hardest thing she'd ever do. Yet she chose to talk about God's goodness anyway. "And they worshiped the Lord there" (1 Samuel 1:28b).

Beautiful girl, as you remember God's goodness, the voice of comparison will grow quiet. God loves to hear us tell all about our good news. Let's celebrate what He has done for us.

we silence the VOICE of COMPARISON by REMEMBERING GOD'S goodness

JOURNAL

Doodle

WEEK
FOUR

Day 16
THE WEIRD ONE

My heart is confident in you, O God; my heart is confident.
No wonder I can sing your praises!

— Psalm 57:7

I COULD BARELY MAKE OUT THE WHISPERS OF "HERE COMES THE weird one," as Karah strutted into the classroom. She never seemed to be in a hurry, never worried about being tardy. She was just carefree and joyful.

That boho-style skirt she always wore drew jeers and teasing from the popular kids. She was different for sure. She even *sat at her desk* differently from everyone else. But Karah didn't care about what others thought. That's what made her so unique. Not just her style or her attitude, but her confidence in herself through the eyes of her Savior.

> *"My heart is confident in you, O God; my heart is confident.*
> *No wonder I can sing your praises!"*
>
> — Psalm 57:7

I always felt inspired by Karah's confidence. In junior high, my friends' opinions mattered most to me. If someone had made a joke about my favorite skirt, I would never have worn it again! Not Karah though. She didn't allow what others thought to change who she was. That reminds me of another teenager named Rhoda. People talked about her too, but she didn't lose her joy.

"...he (Peter) went to the home of Mary, the mother of John Mark, where many were gathered for prayer. He knocked at the door in the gate, and a servant girl named Rhoda came to open it. When she recognized Peter's voice, she was so overjoyed that, instead of opening the door, she ran back inside and told everyone, 'Peter is standing at the door!'"
— Acts 12:12-14

It was a treacherous time for the Christian church. One of their leaders had been killed, and now Peter sat in prison, awaiting his fate. A group of believers gathered at a woman named Mary's house and prayed all night long. Until someone knocked at the door.

Were they scared? Panicked? Mary's young servant Rhoda went to the door and instantly recognized Peter's voice. She was so excited, she ran to tell everyone. But instead of believing and joining in her joyful praise, they called her crazy.

"You're out of your mind!" they said. When she insisted, they decided, "It must be his angel."
— Acts 12:15

Just like my friend Karah, Rhoda knew the sting of being called *the weird one*. Yet notice how she responded. She didn't try to change or fit into their image. She insisted with confidence. She stayed true to herself.

That brings us to the faith statement for today.

BEING CONFIDENT IN WHO GOD SAYS I AM HELPS ME RELEASE THE NEED TO MEASURE UP.

So why does God want us to have confidence? Like every good gift from Him, it has a specific purpose—to do His will. God's Word says in Hebrews 10:35-36, "Therefore do not cast away your confidence, which has great reward. For you have need of endurance, so that after you have done the will of God, you may receive the promise" (NKJV).

God doesn't want us to be someone we're not, and He definitely doesn't want us to be an exact replica of someone else. Let's be encouraged by Karah and Rhoda today. When someone calls us *the weird one*, let's remember what God says about us. We are chosen. We are wonderful. We are His.

Beautiful girl, remain confident in who God says you are, what He says you can do, and what He has for you. Only then will you be able to release the need to measure up.

Day 17
THE QUIET, CONFIDENT ONE

Put on your new nature, created to be like God—
truly righteous and holy.

— EPHESIANS 4:24

IF I ASKED YOU TO THINK OF THE MOST CONFIDENT PERSON YOU KNOW, who would it be? Would you think of someone like my friend Karah from yesterday? Or would it be someone you'd describe as an extrovert—a person who enters a room and draws all the attention with her witty jokes and outgoing nature?

You might be surprised if I told you God defines confidence in a totally different way than we do. And as we learn more about His definition, we will discover that having quiet confidence can be the best type of all.

"Put on your new nature, created to be like God—truly righteous and holy."

— EPHESIANS 4:24

There was a young lady in the Bible who knew all about having quiet confidence. We don't even know her name, but she let her bold faith shine through her gentle and compassionate nature. We only know her as a maid to the wife of a man called Namaan. He had leprosy, and his suffering brought great anguish to his wife. She loved him so much and didn't want him to hurt.

One day this meek young slave, who had been stolen from her home and family in a time of war, offered a daring suggestion—that Namaan should go see the prophet Elisha.

"One day the girl said to her mistress, 'I wish my master would go to see the prophet in Samaria. He would heal him of his leprosy.'"

— 2 KINGS 5:3

In those days, it would be out of line for a slave to speak out like that, so we can tell she had developed a relationship of respect with Namaan's wife. Rather than punishing her, Namaan followed her advice. He visited the prophet, followed his orders, and was healed.

Sometimes being the confident one simply means doing our best each day to live in a way that honors God. Sure, we will mess up sometimes. But as we follow His command to show patience, kindness, and faithfulness, we will develop a Christ-like confidence that can be seen by those around us. Our faith statement today is this.

WE CAN SHOW CHRIST-LIKE CONFIDENCE BY LIVING IN A WAY THAT HONORS GOD.

When we do our best to honor God, we will earn the respect of the people God has placed in our lives. Then as He asks us to step out in bold faith, we will be ready. "Because of Christ and our faith in him, we can now come boldly and confidently into God's presence" (Ephesians 3:12).

Beautiful girl, quiet confidence is okay with God.

Day 18
FRIENDSHIP OVER FOLLOWERS

Don't look out only for your own interests,
but take an interest in others, too.

— PHILIPPIANS 2:4

THE SOUNDS OF MORNING BASKETBALL PRACTICE ECHO THROUGH THE
gym. A few early birds are lined up for layups at one end of the
court. Camryn takes a break and jogs over to Nakyah who is sitting on the bottom row of bleachers recording her teammates with
her phone.

"You better put your phone away so you don't get in trouble.
Coach will be out here any minute," Camryn warns.

"No worries. Coach asked me to video our layups for our
meeting after school. She says it'll help us improve our form."

Camryn nods as Bailey, the team manager, emerges from the
locker room with an armful of basketballs. One ball falls causing
Bailey to trip, and she lands face-first on the floor with balls roll-
ing in every direction. Bailey smiles and blushes while the group
laughs.

"Sweet! I can't believe I just caught that on video! I can't wait to get home today and post it. This thing is going to go viral." Nakyah shouts, "Hey, Bailey! You're going to be an internet sensation!" Only Camryn notices Bailey's concerned look.

Later at lunch, the three girls gather at their usual table. Nakyah passes around the phone, showing off her video. "Bailey, you're hilarious. I'm going to have like a million followers after I post this." Bailey offers a forced giggle and gets up to leave.

When the bell rings, Camryn feels conflicted about what to do. "*Should I talk to Nakyah? Or mind my own business?*" Camryn wonders. But even though she tries to ignore it, a voice keeps repeating in her head. *Friendship.*

"Hey, Nakyah, wait up," Camryn calls out. "Do you think it's a good idea to post that video? I mean, Bailey didn't look too happy about it."

"What do you mean? She was laughing too," Nakyah reasons.

"All I'm saying is maybe you should put yourself in Bailey's shoes. How would you feel if that was you in the video? You and Bailey have been friends for a long time. Do you want to jeopardize that for a few followers? At least talk to her about it before you decide, okay?" Camryn leaves Nakyah to think about it, hoping she hadn't sounded bossy. Maybe Nakyah will listen to her and pause before she posts.

After school, the team hustles out to the court at the sound of the coach's whistle, leaving only Bailey and Nakyah still getting ready in the locker room. Nakyah remembers Camryn's words and turns toward her friend. "Bailey, be honest with me. How do you feel about me posting that video of you falling?"

"Not too great, really," Bailey answers.

"Then why didn't you tell me?"

"At first I didn't think it was a big deal." Bailey goes on, "but the more I thought about it, the more nervous I got. I mean, it's fine for our friends to think it's funny, but that's different than hundreds of strangers laughing at me. That would be pretty embarrassing."

"Yeah, I guess so. I would never do anything to hurt you, Bailey. You're my friend, and that comes first. Besides, I'd choose friendship over followers any day." Nakyah takes out her phone and shows Bailey, "Here, I'm deleting the video right now."

The two friends trot out the door arm-in-arm. Nakyah holds up her phone, and the two stop to pose. "How about a picture together?" she asks.

"Sure! Now that's something you *can* post," Bailey quips.

Today's faith statement comes from our fictional story of three good friends.

LET'S AGREE TO CHOOSE FRIENDSHIP OVER FOLLOWERS.

Our devo about Camryn, Nakyah, and Bailey reminds us always to put others before ourselves. Philippians 2:4 says, "Don't look out only for your own interests, but take an interest in others, too." When we're tempted to do something that could cause a problem for someone else, let's remember the value of good friends.

Beautiful girl, being a good friend brings blessings to you and others.

Day 19
FOR EVERY GIRL

For God so loved the world that he gave his one and only Son, that whoever believes in him shall not perish but have eternal life.

— JOHN 3:16 NIV

FLIPPING BACK THROUGH THE PAGES OF THIS BOOK, I CAN'T HELP BUT notice all the mistakes and mess-ups I've confessed. Some stories brought us laughter; others were more painful. But I felt comfortable telling them to you. Because the truth is, we all fall short of perfect. We all mess up.

"for all have sinned and fall short of the glory of God..."
— ROMANS 3:23 NIV

It took me a while to accept this. When I first read Genesis 1:27, "So God created human beings in His own image," I got worried. God's image? I *definitely* fell short of that. And the more I tried to live up to what I thought I needed to be, I got down on myself, afraid I would disappoint God. I wondered how He could love someone who messed up so often and couldn't seem to get it right. But then I learned something astounding, and I'd like to share it with you.

> ## GOD'S LOVE ISN'T DETERMINED BY MY IMPERFECTIONS. HE SEALED HIS LOVE ON MY HEART THROUGH JESUS.

"For God so loved the world that he gave his one and only Son, that whoever believes in him shall not perish but have eternal life."
— JOHN 3:16 NIV

Maybe you picked up this book already understanding how much God loves you. Maybe you needed something in your life to change, but you couldn't quite figure out what. Or maybe—just maybe—someone handed you this book and you opened it not knowing (or even caring) what it was about.

Can I tell you something, beautiful girl? I fully believe with my whole heart, God brought you to these words right now. You are not reading them by accident. And as you scan this page, I'm praying for you. Praying you will feel a tugging inside that won't let go, the same tug I felt when God wanted me to find a love unlike anything I'd ever felt before—the love of His perfect son Jesus.

If you feel that tugging right now, pray this prayer with me:

Dear God,

Thank you for loving me just the way I am. I am sorry that I mess up sometimes, but I know you love me anyway. Thank you for forgiving me and for sending Jesus to earth to die for my sins. I want Jesus to come into my heart and be with me forever so I can have eternal life with You. Amen.

A note from me to you

I've loved our time together, learning from God's Word and talking about trading comparison for the true me. I almost want to stop you from turning the page because I know it's our last devo! But even though we near the end of the book, your bright future is just beginning. Let Jesus lead the way.

"Furthermore, because we are united with Christ, we have received an inheritance from God, for he chose us in advance, and he makes everything work out according to his plan" (Ephesians 1:11).

Remember that God's love for you overflows. You are always in His heart and mine,

Kristine

Day 20
THE TRUE YOU

*For we are God's masterpiece. He has created us anew in Christ
Jesus, so we can do the good things he planned for us long ago.*

— EPHESIANS 2:10

REMEMBER THE DAY I SAT IN FRONT OF THAT LIGHTED VANITY MIRROR
and answered a question which invited comparison into my life?
The well-meaning beauty expert called on each girl to examine
herself and decide what she would change if she could.

Imagine yourself there with me, all of us lined up in seats
facing the mirror. Just the name "vanity mirror" makes me cringe.
The word *vanity* can mean, "excessive pride in one's appearance, or
conceit," but a *vanity mirror* is simply a tool used in theater to create the lighting needed for applying the right amount of makeup.
A row of ultra-bright lights lines the top of the mirror, exposing
every detail.

That's what made it so easy to compare myself to the other girls that day. Those glaring lights seemed to mock me. They
pointed out my obvious imperfections while highlighting others'

pretty features. Without even realizing it, I let the wrong kind of light determine my value. I focused on what needed to change instead of what God deemed beautiful.

> *"For we are God's masterpiece. He has created us anew in Christ Jesus, so we can do the good things he planned for us long ago."*
> — EPHESIANS 2:10

1 John 1:5 reminds us of the one true Light. "This is the message we heard from Jesus and now declare to you: God is light, and there is no darkness in him at all." When we continue to turn our faces toward the Light that is Jesus, we will find the beauty inside. The beauty God designed before we were even born. Let's pay special attention to our final faith statement.

THE LIGHT OF JESUS REVEALS MY TRUE BEAUTY.

As our world discovers more and more ways to compare, cover up, or change our true selves, let's hold tight to this message. Don't erase your amazingness by being like someone else. There is no one on earth like you. The more you allow God's light to shine on you, the more you will see yourself as the masterpiece He created.

Beautiful girl, come closer to Jesus. He determines the true you. Valuable. Special. Amazing.

the

light

of

Jesus

reveals

my True

Beauty

Journal

Doodle

Some quotes, passages, and stories in *Over It. Trading Comparison for the True Me* are taken from the author's original version for women, *Over It. Conquering Comparison to Live Out God's Plan.* These excerpts are used with permission.

About the Author

KRISTINE BROWN WEAVES WORDS TOGETHER IN A WAY THAT DRAWS readers into the adventures and lessons she shares. Her conversational tone and in-depth Scripture studies leave a lasting impact on her audience.

Kristine is a writer, pastor's wife, life-long educator, and mentor. She loves connecting today's women and teen girls with the women of the Bible through our shared experiences. Kristine finds her greatest joy in being a wife, mom, and Mimi. She lives in Texas with her husband and her dog, Bandit.

Kristine is a contributing writer for *Unlocked for Teens*. You can read or listen to more daily devotions for teens by downloading the Unlocked app.

Find Kristine online at *www.morethanyourself.com*.

Special Thanks

I would like to extend a special "thank you" to Jana Kennedy-Spicer of Sweet to the Soul Ministries for the uniquely designed coloring, journaling, and doodling pages.

You can find more of Jana's fabulous creations at her website, *SweetToTheSoul.com*, and her Etsy shop, *SweetToTheSoulShoppe.com*.

www.ingramcontent.com/pod-product-compliance
Lightning Source LLC
Chambersburg PA
CBHW051732040426
42447CB00008B/1091